Solo Standards for Piano

Eight Elegant Jazz Piano Arrangements

Volume 2: Songs of 1929

by Jeremy Siskind

With Guest Arrangements by:

Xavier Davis

Kevin Hays

Geoffrey Keezer

Helen Sung

Engraving by Kim Groves Brand

Cover & Design by Kelly DiBernardo Rupert

ISBN: 979-8-9874806-8-7

Visit Jeremy Siskind online at

www.jeremysiskind.com

Table of Contents

From the Author

In 2024, I published *Solo Standards for Piano (Book 1),* which included eight of my own arrangements of standards from 1928. This year, I decided to seek inspiration and expertise from four incredible friends. In addition to my four arrangements, this book features four arrangements by four modern jazz piano masters. Playing through their arrangements, I found myself newly in awe of what the piano can do!

This edition features songs from 1929, a pivotal year in world history, which marked the beginning of the Great Depression. Despite the coming news – the stock market didn't crash until the end of October – the dominant style of many songs from 1929 is noticeably upbeat, happy, and optimistic. Fats Waller's carefree manner dominates the year, and some of his greatest hits, "Ain't Misbehavin,'" "Black and Blue," and "Honeysuckle Rose" all written in collaboration with lyricist Andy Razaf, date from 1929. Other happy songs could almost have been written by Waller – "I Guess I'll Have to Change My Plan," "Just a Gigolo," "Can't We Be Friends," "Mean to Me," "Should I," and others – all have that "Roaring Twenties" feeling of carefree optimism.

And then, there is Cole Porter. Two of Porter's earliest entries into the Great American Songbook, "What is This Thing Called Love" and "You Do Something from Me" date from 1929. If most other composers sound rosy and optimistic in the manner of the "Roaring Twenties," Cole Porter always sounds like himself, mixing major and minor keys into a wholly original concoction. His unpredictable harmonic palette, ribald sense of humor, and insistence on going his own way make his songs stand out from the crowd.

This book comes with online resources accessible at **https://jeremysiskind.com/standards1929/** or by scanning the QR code on the right. Included on the webpage, you'll find:

- video recordings of my own performances of these arrangements
- recordings of each guest arranger performing their arrangement
- PDFs of the arrangements with chord symbols above the staff for study

Finally, if you would like to learn how to create your own jazz piano arrangements and solos, I have written several books explaining jazz theory, practice techniques, and solo piano arranging. You can purchase *Playing Solo Jazz Piano* and the *Jazz Piano Fundamentals* series at **www.jeremysiskind.com/shop/** or by scanning the QR code to the right. Use the code "1929Book" for a special discount!

Please enjoy these arrangements! If you're proud of your performances, I'd love to hear them. Send a video or recording of your performance to me at **info@jeremysiskind.com**. Happy playing!

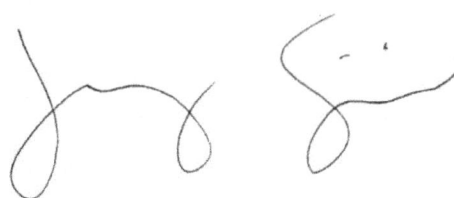

Jeremy Siskind

About the Guest Arrangers

Helen Sung is an award-winning jazz pianist and composer and a Guggenheim Fellow. A native of Houston, Texas, and alumna of HSPVA, she diverged from her classical upbringing after a jazz epiphany during studies at the University of Texas at Austin. Helen went on to graduate in the inaugural class of the Thelonious Monk Institute of Jazz Performance (re-named the Herbie Hancock Institute) and win the Kennedy Center's Mary Lou Williams Piano Competition. In addition to her own band and projects, she has performed with such luminaries as Clark Terry, Wayne Shorter, Ron Carter, Wynton Marsalis, Regina Carter, Terri Lyne Carrington, Cecile McLorin Salvant, and the Mingus Big Band. She is currently on faculty at the San Francisco Conservatory of Music and Columbia University, where she also was the first jazz artist-in-residence at its Mortimer B. Zuckerman Mind Brain Behavior Institute exploring intersections of jazz and neuroscience. Helen is a Steinway Artist.

Geoffrey Keezer is a GRAMMY®-winning pianist, composer, arranger and producer based in New York City. A native of Eau Claire, Wisconsin, he began playing piano and composing at an early age. After briefly attending the Berklee College of Music in Boston, Keezer moved to New York in 1989, becoming the last pianist with the legendary Art Blakey and the Jazz Messengers. Keezer has toured and recorded with Ray Brown, Roy Hargrove, Joshua Redman, Diana Krall, Art Farmer, Benny Golson, Barbara Hendricks, Wayne Shorter, Dianne Reeves, David Sanborn, Chris Botti, Sting, Joe Locke and Christian McBride. Geoffrey Keezer is a faculty member of The Juilliard School and is a Yamaha artist.

Xavier Davis' professional career as a jazz pianist took off when the legendary vocalist Betty Carter spotted his outstanding talent at the 1994 International Association of Jazz Educators convention in Boston while he was performing with his college ensemble. Carter herself brought Xavier to New York, hiring him exclusively as the pianist of her working trio. Today, Xavier is one of the most accomplished jazz pianists in the world. Having led master classes and clinics all over the world and coming from a family of music educators, passing on knowledge and skills to young musicians is very important to Xavier. As such, he is proud to be Associate Professor of Jazz Piano at Michigan State University. Xavier was also member of the teaching staff in the Jazz department of the Juilliard School of Music in New York for six years.

Grammy Award-winning jazz pianist, composer, and singer/songwriter **Kevin Hays**'s many recordings have received critical acclaim from *The New York Times*, *Downbeat Magazine* and *Jazz Times*, as well as the "Coup de Coeur" award from the Académie Charles Cros (France).

Kevin has appeared on numerous albums as a guest artist, recording with Chris Potter, Bill Stewart, Joshua Redman, Jeff Ballard, Nicholas Payton, and Al Foster, among many others. Notable collaborations include a piano duo project with Brad Mehldau (*Modern Music* - Nonesuch), world tours with James Taylor, Sonny Rollins, John Scofield, Joe Henderson, and Roy Haynes.

Notes on Markings

Choosing how much articulation, dynamics, and pedaling notation to include is one of the most stressful aspects of writing a book of piano music. If the arranger includes too much specificity, the page becomes a mess, and the player can become overwhelmed. But if the author includes too little, the page can look random, and the player might feel that they lack guidance on style.

I did not change the markings of my guest arrangers. Any markings you see from them are original and, for this reason, each of the arrangements will have a slightly different style of articulation.

Here are a few explanations about the decisions I made about markings that will help you navigate these arrangements.

Articulation

Quite a lot of articulation is included in the book in order to help pianists who are less familiar with swing feel achieve better jazz articulation.

- Slurs generally indicate legato touch in swing pieces and phrase markings in ballads and straight-eighth note pieces.

- Consecutive notes not marked with other articulation should generally be played legato, even if they are not marked with a slur.

- Tenutos (-) are used to indicate two main categories of notes: (1) quarter notes in a swing feel, mostly on the beat, that should be played long but not connected ("daht" articulation) and (2) longer notes with mild accents, adding a bit of extra weight without creating a harsh accent.

- The accent marking (<) indicates a harsher, more distinct accent, usually in the middle of a phrase or for a longer note.

- The triangle/ "caret" marking (∧) indicates a percussive accent, which should be played staccato and loud. This marking usually accompanies an offbeat eighth note that ends a phrase.

- Staccato markings (.) are rarely used here. When a staccato marking appears, it indicates a short note to be played particularly lightly, with no accent at the end of a phrase.

- Passages in which the pianist's left hand imitates a bassline are generally marked with the word "legato" to indicate that there should be no silence in between left-hand notes.

Use your own musicality, knowledge of style, and reference the video recordings that accompany the book to inform your decisions regarding articulation.

Fingering

I have tried to share fingerings that will be helpful, especially within single-note melodic lines. All fingerings are written with my hands in mind and there are no "definitive" fingering solutions. Therefore, if you find another fingering that feels more comfortable, please don't feel obligated to use my suggestion.

I did add some of my own fingerings to my guest arrangers' pieces when I thought there was a clear "best way" to finger the passage.

Pedal

I have broadly marked where the pedal should be used more lightly or more heavily. In a swing context, less pedal is almost always preferred because pedal muddies articulation and accents. When playing in a swing rhythm, use only short pedals to connect between adjacent chords that can't possibly be connected with the fingers. Whenever possible, make connections with the fingers to preserve the option of percussive articulation.

Dynamics

Most jazz music is not known for dramatic dynamic contrasts, but some shaping is necessary, especially on the ballads and straight-eighth note pieces. I have included some dynamic suggestions but feel free to shape using your own musical instincts.

Most of the dynamics on guest arrangers' submissions are original, but occasionally I added dynamics in an effort to create a consistent style.

Chord Symbols

Chord symbols are not included in these scores in an effort to prevent the page from becoming overly crowded. However, three versions with chord symbols are included on the webpage for this book:

- the first version shows just the "original" chord changes, the ones that are found on the leadsheet
- the second version shows the chords implied by the arrangement
- the third version shows both the "original" chord changes and the chords implied by the arrangement. The third version is meant to be useful for students studying jazz harmony and reharmonization.

Smart, thoughtful people can disagree about the best ways to name chords. I have done my best to name these chords in a way that will be useful, concise, and easy to read, but it is easy to imagine many possible solutions for nearly every measure of these arrangements.

Section Markings

To help less experienced jazz students recognize the format of the arrangements, sections like introductions, endings, heads, and solos are marked with boxed text. Hopefully, these markings help keep the pianist oriented and help students analyze how each part of the piece contributes to creating a satisfying whole.

About the Arrangements

Liza

"Liza" holds an important place in the history of jazz piano. Its privileged status was established through virtuosic recordings by James P. Johnson and Art Tatum and cemented with classic renditions by Nat "King" Cole and Oscar Peterson. Later, "Liza" was reinterpreted with vastly different harmony by Thelonious Monk. Perhaps this history explains why Herbie Hancock and Chick Corea decided to feature such an unabashedly "classic-sounding" song on their decidedly modern-sounding album *An Evening with Herbie Hancock and Chick Corea*.

The version in this book features the original harmonization for the first two A sections and Monk's reharmonization for the final A section. The leadsheet version in the appendix compares three historically important harmonizations. Look for closed-position and drop-two voicings during the head and "shell stride" in the bridge, an accompaniment style in which the left-hand voicings are divided between the root and the shell to create a "stride piano" effect that avoids big hand movements.

More Than You Know

When Frank Sinatra introduces "More Than You Know" on his live album, *Standing Room Only*, he says that the song was "written in protest when songs were dull." Presumably, he meant that the song was written as a response to the banality of popular songs of the '20s. Indeed, "More Than You Know" offers many satisfying and inventive twists and turns.

This arrangement of "More Than You Know" presents the piece as a medium-tempo, lilting jazz waltz, rather than the typical jazz-ballad format. The left hand uses a "shuttle" technique, alternating between low bass notes and mid-range chords. Shuttle is similar to stride, but whereas stride requires a new left-hand chord every beat, shuttle can be syncopated and unpredictable.

Without a Song

Written by the same team as "More Than You Know," "Without a Song" is a popular song among jazz instrumentalists. Perhaps the definitive recording for instrumentalists is from Sonny Rollins' 1962 album, *The Bridge*, featuring Jim Hall on guitar.

Kevin Hays' version is filled with beauty and mystery. Be sure to listen to the composers' version on the webpage for this book to hear how he plays with razor-sharp focus, always bringing out the melody and staying connected to the lyric, which can be found in the appendix.

You Do Something to Me

Cole Porter's first fully integrated book musical, *Fifty Million Frenchmen*, featured the song "You Do Something to Me," which has since been recorded by a wide range of performers including Frank Sinatra, Ella Fitzgerald, Bing Crosby, Lena Horne, and João Gilberto. The song features harmonic and rhythmic surprises, especially during the famous lines "Do, do that voodoo that you do so well," which seems to be in "double time" and a different key compared to the rest of the tune.

Helen Sung takes the idea of the double-time section and runs with it. Her arrangement features several fascinating yet intuitive changes of tempo and mood, which accentuate Porter's daring composition. Playing her version feels like a rollicking roller coaster ride, with bursts of drama, color, and surprises included.

What Is This Thing Called Love?

The other famous Porter tune from 1929 is a cornerstone of the jazz standard repertoire. Not only do jazz musicians love playing the original melody, but they also love playing other melodies written over the same chord progression ("contrafacts"), like Tadd Dameron's "Hot House," Lee Konitz's "Subconscious Lee," and John Coltrane's "Fifth House." The harmony is fascinating for musicians because its first chord (G half diminished seventh in the key of C) is very distant from its eventual tonic key of C major.

Geoffrey Keezer's arrangement is a technicolor delight. Nearly every measure features some new and exciting, unpredictable and daring, pianistic device. Interestingly, Keezer places the verse in the middle of the tune instead of at the beginning, where it traditionally belongs. Admire the ways in which Keezer hints at "symmetrical scales" like the octatonic and whole-tone scales, while incorporating other notes to create entirely new chord and scale colors.

Honeysuckle Rose

One of the most commonly performed songs in the jazz repertoire, "Honeysuckle Rose" is a favorite of both vocalists and instrumentalists. To get inspired for this arrangement, I listened to Fats Waller's 1956 recording and was stunned by Waller's harmonic inventiveness. Rather than using the standard ii-V-I harmony, Waller harmonizes his tune with sophisticated passing chords without sacrificing any of the color. This arrangement should be easily recognizable to lovers of the tune while avoiding the most overused clichés.

Stardust

Though written in 1927 and recorded in 1928, "Stardust" was not technically published until 1929, hence its inclusion in this edition. A haunting ballad, "Stardust" is one of the rare jazz standards for which musicians almost *have* to include the beautiful verse. Although there are too many classic recordings to list, Nat "King" Cole's was the most direct inspiration for this arrangement.

Like Cole's version, my arrangement seeks to reflect the magic of the lyric. The Debussy-inspired chords in the introduction and ending aim to conjure images of stars dotting the night sky. Much of this arrangement references Hank Jones' beautiful interpretation of "The Very Thought of You," which also features a "Peace Piece" left hand and rolled octaves in the upper register of the right hand. In the second half, the high octaves responding to the melody reflect Rachmaninoff's beautiful Prelude in D major.

Gee Baby, Ain't I Good to You

"Gee Baby" is "bluesy" with a capital "B"! In addition to music by Don Redman, this song features lyrics by Andy Razaf, Fats Waller's frequent collaborator. I highly recommend researching a biography of Razaf, who led a fascinating life. He was related to kings and queens of the Imerina kingdom in Africa who fled the French invasion of Madagascar to find safety in the U.S.

"Gee Baby" is an unusual jazz standard because of its short form, only sixteen measures instead of thirty-two, and the fact that it harmonically starts so far from the tonic. Its bluesy, conversational melody is hard to notate with precise fidelity for the piano, but both the arrangement and the leadsheet use a combination of triplets and ornaments to achieve a vocal style.

Xavier Davis' arrangement takes the traditional "down-home and dirty blues" feel to school! Stride, march, and Freddie Green-style left hand patterns are combined with unexpected reharmonizations, playful double-time lines, and expressive ornaments to create a memorable, colorful, and fun-to-play version. If rolling the voicings that span a tenth proves to be a burden, feel free to omit the bottom note to make those voicings more manageable.

Liza

George Gershwin/Ira Gershwin/Gus Kahn
Arranged by Jeremy Siskind

with sparse pedal

To Coda ⊕

Solo

non-legato, no pedal

More Than You Know

Victor Youmans, William Rose, Edward Eliscu
Arranged by Jeremy Siskind

Verse

Freely and Fluidly (♩ = 92)

with pedal

with sparse or no pedal

Without a Song

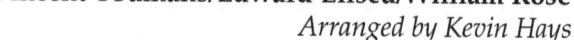

Vincent Youmans/Edward Eliscu/William Rose
Arranged by Kevin Hays

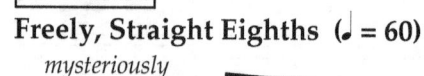

Freely, Straight Eighths (♩ = 60)

You Do Something to Me

Cole Porter

Arranged by Helen Sung

Head Out (Second Half)
Più mosso (straight 8ths)

improvisatory flourish

Espressivo (straight 8ths)

improvisatory flourish

What Is This Thing Called Love?

Cole Porter

Arranged by Geoffrey Keezer

Honeysuckle Rose

Fats Waller/Andy Razaf
Arranged by Jeremy Siskind

Stardust

Hoagy Carmichael
Arranged by Jeremy Siskind

Gee Baby, Ain't I Good To You

Don Redman/Andy Razaf
Arranged by Xavier Davis

with minimal pedal

Head Out (with Variation)

Appendix

Liza

Music: George Gershwin
Lyrics: Ira Gershwin and Gus Kahn

Liza, Liza, skies are gray
But if you'll smile on me
All the clouds'll roll away

Liza, Liza, don't delay
Come keep me company
And the clouds'll roll away

See the honeymoon a-shinin' down
We should make a date with Parson Brown

So Liza, Liza, name the day
When you belong to me
And the clouds'll roll away

Liza

George Gershwin/Ira Gershwin/Gus Kahn

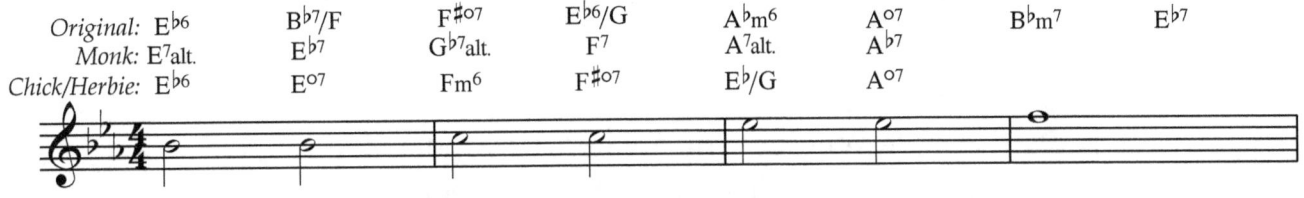

More Than You Know

Music: Vincent Youmans
Lyrics: William Rose and Edward Eliscu

Verse
Whether you are here or yonder
Whether you are false or true
Whether you remain or wander
I'm growing fonder of you
Even though your friends forsake you
Even though you don't succeed
Wouldn't I be glad to take you
Give you the break you need

Refrain
More than you know, more than you know
Man of my heart I love you so
Lately I find you're on my mind
More than you know

Whether you're right, whether you're wrong
Man of my heart, I'll string along
You need me so
Much more than you'll ever know

Loving you the way that I do
There's nothing I can do about it
Loving may be all you can give
But, honey, I can't live without it

Oh how I'd sigh, oh how I'd cry
If you got tired and said goodbye
More than I'd show
More than you'll ever know

More Than You Know

Vincent Youmans/William Rose/Edward Eliscu

Without a Song

Music: Vincent Youmans
Lyrics: William Rose and Edward Eliscu

Without a song the day would never end
Without a song the road would never bend
When things go wrong, a man ain't got a friend
Without a song

That field of corn would never see a plough
That field of corn would be deserted now
A young one's born but he's no good no how
Without a song

I got my trouble and woe but sure as I know
The Jordan will roll
I'll get along as long as a song
Is strung in my soul

I'll never know what makes the rain to fall
I'll never know what makes the grass so tall
I only know there ain't no love at all
Without a song

Without a Song

Vincent Youmans/William Rose/Edward Eliscu

You Do Something to Me

Music and Lyrics: Cole Porter

You do something to me
Something that simply mystifies me

Tell me, why should it be
You have the power to hypnotize me

Let me live 'neath your spell
Do, do that voodoo that you do so well

For you do something to me
That nobody else could do

You Do Something to Me

Cole Porter

What Is This Thing Called Love?

Music and Lyrics: Cole Porter

Verse
I was a humdrum person
Leading a life apart
When love flew in through my window wide
And quickened my humdrum heart

Love flew in through my window
I was so happy then
But after love had stayed a little while
Love flew out again

Refrain
What is this thing called love?
This funny thing xalled love?

Just who can solve its mystery?
Why should it make a fool of me?

I saw you there
One wonderful day
You took my heart
And threw it away

That's why I ask the lord In heaven above
What is this thing called love?

What Is This Thing Called Love?

Cole Porter

Honeysuckle Rose

Music: Fats Waller
Lyrics: Andy Razaf

Every honeybee fills with jealousy
When they see you out with me
Goodness knows
You're my honeysuckle rose

When you're passin' by flowers droop and sigh
And I know the reason why
Goodness knows
You're my honeysuckle rose

Don't buy sugar
You just have to touch my cup
You're my sugar
It's sweeter when you stir it up

When I'm taking sips from your tasty lips
Seems the honey fairly drips
Goodness knows
You're my honeysuckle rose

Honeysuckle Rose

Fats Waller / Andy Razaf

Stardust

Music and Lyrics: Hoagy Carmichael

Verse
And now the purple dusk of twilight time
Steals across the meadows of my heart
High up in the sky the little stars climb
Always reminding me that we're apart

You wander down the lane and far away
Leaving me a song that will not die
Love is now the stardust of yesterday
The music of the years gone by

Refrain
Sometimes I wonder why I spend
The lonely night dreaming of a song
The melody haunts my reverie
And I am once again with you
When our love was new
And each kiss an inspiration
But that was long ago
Now my consolation
Is in the stardust of a song

Beside a garden wall
When stars are bright
You are in my arms
The nightingale tells his fairytale
Of paradise where roses bloom
Though I dream in vain
In my heart it will remain
My stardust melody
The memory of love's refrain

Stardust

Hoagy Carmichael

Gee Baby, Ain't I Good to You

Music: Don Redman
Lyrics: Andy Razaf

What makes me treat you the way that I do?
Gee baby, ain't I good to you

There's nothing too good for a girl that's good and true
Gee baby, ain't I good to you

I bought you a fur coat for Christmas, a diamond ring
A big Cadillac car and everything

Love makes me treat you the way that I do
Gee baby, ain't I good to you

Gee Baby, Ain't I Good to You

Don Redman / Andy Razaf